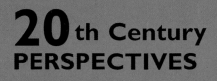

20th Century
PERSPECTIVES

The Changing Role of Women

Mandy Ross

Heinemann
LIBRARY

H www.heinemann.co.uk
Visit our website to find out more information about Heinemann Library books.

To order:
☎ Phone 44 (0) 1865 888066
▤ Send a fax to 44 (0) 1865 314091
▢ Visit the Heinemann Bookshop at www.heinemann.co.uk to browse our catalogue and order online.

First published in Great Britain by Heinemann Library,
Halley Court, Jordan Hill, Oxford OX2 8EJ,
a division of Reed Educational and Professional Publishing Ltd.
Heinemann is a registered trademark of Reed Educational and Professional Publishing Ltd.

OXFORD MELBOURNE AUCKLAND
JOHANNESBURG BLANTYRE GABORONE
IBADAN PORTSMOUTH (NH) USA CHICAGO

© Reed Educational and Professional Publishing Ltd 2002
The moral right of the proprietor has been asserted.

Produced for Heinemann Library by Discovery Books Limited
Designed by Ian Winton
Consultant: Kate Nash
Originated by Dot Gradations
Printed by Wing King Tong in Hong Kong

ISBN 0 431 11997 X
05 04 03 02
10 9 8 7 6 5 4 3 2 1

British Library Cataloguing in Publication Data
Ross, Mandy, 1963 –
  The changing role of women. – (20th century perspectives)
  1.Women – History – 20th century – Juvenile literature
  2.Women – Social conditions – 20th century – Juvenile literature
  I.Title
  305.4'2'0904

Acknowledgements
The publishers would like to thank the following for permission to reproduce photographs:
Bettmann/Corbis pp. 12, 22, 24, 27, 28; Corbis/Peter Turnley p.16; Corbis/Liba Taylor p. 19; Corbis/David Rubinger p.21; Corbis/Earl and Nazima Kowall p.23; Corbis/Marc Garanger p.35; Corbis/Ann Hawthorn p.40; Hulton Archive Photos/Lewes W Hine p.4; Hulton Archive Photos/Humphrey Spender p.20; Hulton Deutsch Collection Ltd pp. 6, 33; Hulton Deutsch Collection/Corbis pp. 13, 30; Hulton Getty pp. 11, 18, 25, 38; Peter Newark's American Pictures pp. 5, 29, 31; Peter Newark's Historical pictures pp. 7, 8, 9; Panos Pictures/Zed Nelson p. 42; Popperfoto pp. 10, 14, 15, 17, 32, 34, 36, 39 (Jacques Demarthon); Popperfoto/ Reuters pp. 26, 41, 43; Redferns p. 37.

Cover photograph reproduced with permission of Hulton Deutsch Collection/Corbis

The author would like to thank Nesta Ross, Myra Connell and Karen Whiteside for all of their help.

Any words appearing in the text in bold, **like this**, are explained in the glossary.

Contents

Women in 1900

It might be hard for women in the **developed** world today to imagine how vastly different women's lives were in the **West** only a hundred years ago – and how different they still are in many parts of the world. In 1900 most women's lives were spent at the bidding of men. Women were not free to control their own lives, their property or even their own bodies. They were not treated as full adults, but rather like an inferior human group who could not be trusted to make their own decisions.

Women's lives

Without **birth control**, women often had large families, and would spend most of their adult lives pregnant and caring for children. In 1900, almost no women had the vote, so they had no right to question how their country was run. In many countries, women were under the control of their fathers or husbands, who also controlled any money or property they owned. Many women could not live **independently**, because they could not earn a living.

Rich and poor

Rich women's lives were very different from poor women's. In 1900 women in rich families rarely went to work, and lived a life of leisure and boredom, supported by their husbands. In poor families, life for women was very hard. Women worked long hours, often in poor conditions, in factories or out in the fields. Yet despite their long working hours, women were still expected to look after their homes and bring up their children.

Few countries had any kind of **welfare system** in 1900. Families had to look after themselves – and if they could not earn enough money, they went hungry. Women with children, whose husbands had died or left them, were especially vulnerable.

Women immigrants and their children sewing garments in a cramped New York City apartment, early in the 20th century. Around the world, many women worked in dreadful conditions, often for very low wages.

Women in the colonies

In 1900, many countries in Africa and Asia were **colonies**, that is, they were ruled by other nations, such as Britain or France. The people were kept in poor conditions, living in poverty, denied rights and excluded from education or well-paid jobs. Women were described as 'slaves of slaves', under the control of their husbands or fathers, as well as the colonial power.

Call for women's rights

From the 1840s onwards, many women in the Western world had begun to question the old ways. Two such women, Elizabeth Cady Stanton and Lucretia Mott, organized one of the first women's rights conferences in Seneca Falls, New York in 1848, to 'discuss the social, civil and religious conditions of women'. Stanton joined with Susan B Anthony, another campaigner for women's rights, in founding the National Woman Suffrage Association in 1869. These 'new women', as they were called, wanted new rights and freedoms. They questioned old ideas about marriage, sex and family life. **Feminists** (both men and women) believed that every woman should be independent and active and should be treated equally with men. Women should make their own decisions and, most urgently of all, they should have the right to vote.

In some countries women took up arms to fight for their beliefs. These women 'soldaderas' fought against poverty and the power of the landowners in the Mexican revolution which began in 1910.

Women's rights

'Women's rights' means making sure that women can take their part in society, use their skills, and fulfil their potential. The struggle is not only to achieve equal treatment for men and women, but to recognize the value of women and what they do, as well as to overcome barriers to equality at work and in politics. This battle is not complete, and in some parts of the world women's lives are very far from equal.

Fighting for the vote

At the start of the 20th century, very few women around the world had **suffrage**, that is, the right to vote. Without this right, women's views and wishes could be completely ignored – even when governments made decisions affecting women's lives. Women who campaigned for the right to vote were called **suffragists** or **suffragettes**. Not all men had the vote either, and often it was only rich and powerful men that had this right. What is more, many countries were still ruled by unelected monarchs, emperors or dictators. The struggle for universal suffrage was one of the key issues at the start of the 20th century.

Campaigning in the United States

Members of the National Woman Suffrage Association held meetings, bonfires and street dances, and they used new media such as the movies, advertising and commercial radio to build support for women's votes. But progress was disappointingly slow. Also there were tensions between the campaigns for African-American rights and women's suffrage as some African Americans saw women's suffrage as a distraction from the battle for racial equality.

A suffragette procession through London in 1911. Crowds of supporters line the streets to watch the spectacle.

Shock tactics in Britain

Moderate suffragists organized huge processions to call for women's rights, carrying banners and wearing sashes. Crowds of supporters gathered to watch and cheer them, creating a carnival atmosphere. At one procession in London in April 1909, marchers dressed in the clothes of their trades – to show that women from all backgrounds were united in the suffrage movement: nurses in uniform, poultry farmers carrying baskets of eggs, women from mining communities in shawls, and many others. Famous actresses marched among them.

By 1908, impatient at their lack of progress, the more radical suffragettes in Britain turned to shock tactics. As well as organizing huge demonstrations, they chained themselves to railings, broke windows and stormed the House of

Commons. Many deliberately got themselves arrested and sent to prison to publicize their cause. Some people, and particularly the media, were outraged by these violent tactics and thought they did nothing to further the women's cause.

In prison some suffragettes went on hunger strike and were brutally fed by force, via tubes pushed down their throats. Some were released when they grew weak, only to be re-imprisoned when they had regained their strength. The suffragettes' courage won them widespread admiration amongst men and women of all classes.

The outbreak of World War I

The campaigners for women's suffrage put their cause on hold when World War I broke out in 1914 and instead turned their energy to war work. In many countries this, probably more than anything else, helped them achieve the right to vote, though women in some European countries had to wait until after World War II.

Japanese women in Tokyo calling for the right to vote in 1929. Women did not gain the vote in Japan until 1945.

Women's suffrage around the world

Votes for women was not just a **Western** movement. In 1918, the Women's Indian Association persuaded the newly-formed Indian National Congress to support women's right to vote. In Japan, the Seithoscha feminist group called for suffrage and other rights for women. Meanwhile in China, the Chinese Suffragette Society demanded the vote and political rights for women, and an end to footbinding (where girls' feet were bound and broken so that they could never walk freely). The Egyptian Feminist Union, created in 1923, called for women's votes, funded healthcare and craft workshop projects for poor women and a childcare centre for working mothers.

Mary Wollstonecraft

The struggle for women's rights started long before the 20th century. An Englishwoman, Mary Wollstonecraft, was inspired by the 1789 French Revolution when she wrote *A Vindication of the Rights of Woman* in 1792, arguing for educational and social rights for women.

Women in politics 1914–45

World War I (1914–18) changed people's attitudes towards women. All around the world, women served their country by taking over the work done by the men who had gone off to fight. They proved women could work as hard and as skilfully as men. After the war, women's demand for the vote, once so controversial, seemed much less outrageous. In country after country, women gained the vote. New nations such as Austria, Czechoslovakia and Poland, established in 1918–19 from the break-up of the old empires, introduced women's **suffrage** from the start.

The Hague peace convention

In April 1915, a thousand women peace campaigners from twelve countries met in the Dutch capital, The Hague. They called for an end to the war and for women's right to vote. The Women's International League for Peace and Freedom was formed at The Hague, and still exists today.

Women voters – and politicians

In Britain, women over the age of 30 were granted the vote in 1918 (though it was not until ten years later that all women could vote from the age of 21, the same age as men). US women finally got the vote in 1920. Once they could vote, women started to stand as candidates for election. Ironically the first woman MP to sit in the House of Commons, Nancy Astor, was no great supporter of women's rights. Other early women MPs did try to improve the lot of women, but struggled against the male-dominated agenda and traditions of parliament.

New freedom for women?

As well as the right to vote, the 1920s brought new freedoms and excitement for women in society, such as movies, new jazz music and dancing. Although there was a dazzling array of new consumer goods, such as refrigerators and vacuum cleaners only the rich could afford them for their servants to use. Poor women did not benefit from such labour-saving devices for several decades.

The Russian Revolution brought many changes in women's lives, sometimes for the better. This poster tells women that while they go to work in the Soviet factories, their children will be well cared for in state nurseries.

Women could vote, but because there were very few women active in government little progress was made in terms of women's rights. Some of the opportunities women experienced during the war years were soon lost. In Britain, for example, the Pre-War Practices Act of 1920 excluded women from many skilled jobs, while the Marriage Bar actually banned married women from working in the civil service, local government and many other fields. The Marriage Bar was only dismantled during World War II.

Women and the Russian Revolution

World War I caused terrible hardship in Russia. In 1917, weary of endless queues for rationed bread, the women of Petrograd rioted against food shortages and the loss of life at the front. Men joined the women's riots, which grew and spread until they became a **revolution**, toppling Tsar Nicholas II, and eventually creating a new **communist** nation, the Soviet Union.

Soviet women gained the vote in 1918, though this right was shortlived as they could only vote for one party. Millions of women learned to read and write in a vast **literacy** campaign. They worked alongside men in heavy industry and construction projects, to build their new nation.

A woman working in a munitions factory during World War I. Women's war work helped to earn them the vote in many countries when the war came to an end.

WOMEN'S SUFFRAGE

THIS TABLE SHOWS THE SPREAD OF WOMEN'S SUFFRAGE AROUND THE WORLD. ALTHOUGH WOMEN IN MANY COUNTRIES GAINED THE VOTE AFTER WORLD WAR I, SOME EUROPEAN COUNTRIES SUCH AS FRANCE AND ITALY HELD BACK UNTIL AFTER WORLD WAR II.

1893 NEW ZEALAND	1934 BRAZIL
1902* AUSTRALIA	1937 PHILIPPINES
1906 FINLAND	1944 JAMAICA
1913 NORWAY	1945 FRANCE
1915 DENMARK	1945 ITALY
1917 SOVIET UNION	1945 JAPAN
1918** BRITAIN	1949 CHINA
1918 GERMANY	1949 INDIA
1918 NETHERLANDS	1952 MEXICO
1920 CANADA	1956 EGYPT
1920 USA	1964 KENYA
1932 CEYLON (NOW	1971 SWITZERLAND
SRI LANKA)	1982 JORDAN

* ABORIGINAL WOMEN AND MEN ONLY GAINED THE VOTE IN 1967.

** BRITAIN GRANTED THE VOTE IN 1918 TO WOMEN AGED 30 AND OVER AND TO ALL WOMEN IN 1928.

Eleanor Roosevelt 1884-1962

Eleanor Roosevelt, wife of US President Roosevelt, used her position as First Lady to campaign for the rights of women and African-American people in the USA. She campaigned to improve workers' rights, and worked tirelessly to persuade the **United Nations** to adopt the Universal Declaration of Human Rights in 1948.

Women in politics 1945 onwards

During World War II women were, once again, enlisted to work in the fields and factories of the warring nations, replacing the men who were called up to fight. The years after World War II brought huge changes around the world. Governments adjusted to peace and growing prosperity by setting up **welfare systems**. Many countries in Africa and Asia fought for **independence** from European rule, and gradually a few women were elected as political leaders.

Post-war welfare systems

As economies grew stronger again, many **Western** governments set up welfare policies to make sure that everyone had enough money to live on, free healthcare and education. In Britain, the National Health Service was set up in 1948, and similar systems were introduced in France, West Germany and other Western countries, including Scandinavian nations, Australia and New Zealand. Women benefited from these policies; for instance in Britain child benefit, a weekly allowance paid by the government to help with the cost of raising a family, was paid directly to the mother. Many women worked in the new welfare systems, too, as teachers, nurses and social workers.

Women's role in the fight for independence

After World War II many colonies began to fight for their independence and women played their part in these struggles. In India, for instance, women picketed shops selling foreign goods, spoke at rallies and led demonstrations which helped to bring independence in 1948. In Algeria, women fought alongside their men in the long and bloody struggle to throw off French rule, finally succeeding in 1962. But Algerian women were disappointed that their lives did not change a great deal after independence.

High fliers: women as political leaders

Since the 1960s, individual women have risen to great heights in politics. Mrs Sirimavo Bandaranaike was the first woman to be elected as a national leader when she became prime minister of Sri Lanka in 1960. She was followed in 1966 by Indira Gandhi in

After the assassination of her husband in 1959, Mrs Sirimavo Bandaranaike was elected prime minister of Sri Lanka. This made her the first woman to be elected as a national leader.

Algerian women's liberation?

'We are the daughters of those women who waged a liberation war and whose only liberation was to return to their kitchen.'
Fatma Oussedik, Algerian sociologist, 1984

India and Golda Meir in Israel in 1969. Some of these women, for instance Indira Gandhi, belonged to famous political families whose connections helped them to win votes. But others were elected entirely in their own right.

Margaret Thatcher was Britain's first woman prime minister from 1979 to 1990. In 1997, Madeleine Albright became US Secretary of State. She was the first woman to hold this position and the highest-ranking woman in the history of the US government.

Not all women leaders are champions of women's rights. British prime minister Margaret Thatcher presided over an all-male cabinet, and her government's welfare cuts, especially in maternity benefits, hit poor women hardest.

Getting more women into government

Most traditional political parties are male-dominated and have more men than women among their members. This means that fewer women stand as candidates for election to government. Today the average figure around the world for women in government is only 12.7 per cent.

Political parties in some countries have taken positive action to encourage more women into politics. In Britain, the Labour Party introduced women-only candidate selection shortlists to increase the number of women standing for election. As a result, the Labour government elected in 1997 had a record 101 women MPs (24 per cent), and is trying to cut parliament's long working hours to help women politicians balance their work with their families' needs.

Scandinavian countries have the best record for the number of women in government – around 40 per cent of their elected politicians are women.

International action for women

The **United Nations** (UN) encourages individual governments around the world to work to improve women's rights. In addition to this they have set up projects with the aim of empowering women – that is, giving poor women the tools and skills they need to improve their own lives, rather than waiting for government action. One example is UN support for credit schemes which loan women small amounts of money to start up their own businesses. This builds women's confidence, and also raises their status in their own communities.

Women in civil rights movements

The struggle for racial equality and **civil rights** was a major issue in the 20th century. Women have played an important role in this struggle – though sometimes they have had to stand up for women's rights, too, within these movements. Many linked the struggle for civil rights with that of women's rights. Great progress has been made – but racism and ethnic hatred are still problems in many parts of the world.

Elizabeth Eckford calmly enters Little Rock High School, Arkansas surrounded by protestors and armed guards, September 1957. This attempt at integrating African-Americans into the white school system had to be orded and enforced by the US Federal Court.

Women in the American civil rights movement

In December 1955, an African-American woman, Rosa Parks, was arrested for refusing to give up her seat on the bus to a white man. Her arrest sparked the American civil rights movement, which campaigned for equal rights for African-American people. Protesters met with vicious violence from angry whites. By 1965, **segregation** was banned by law, although some states in the deep south, such as Mississippi and Arkansas, resisted the changes for years.

Risking violence

Supporting the civil rights movement was dangerous. One African-American woman remembers deciding to take that risk, since it seemed that whites had been trying to kill her 'a little bit at a time ever since I could remember'.

South Africa

Meanwhile women in South Africa joined the fight against **apartheid** alongside their men. In 1956, a 20,000-strong women's march protested against the pass laws, which restricted black men and women's freedom to travel. Many women were arrested and imprisoned. Black and mixed-race (called 'coloured') children received only basic education. In the 1950s, school **boycotts** were organized in protest.

Women set up informal schools so that black children would not miss out on their education. Woman also played their part in the political struggle against apartheid. Winnie Mandela was on the executive of the ANC (African National Congress) Women's League. After it was banned many of its women leaders worked within the Federation of South African Women.

Apartheid was finally ended in 1994, when democratic elections were held in South Africa, and Nelson Mandela was elected as president. Now more than a quarter of South African MPs are women, and the government has worked hard to improve women's rights, healthcare and employment conditions.

In Cato Manor near Durban, South Africa, black women riot in protest at government measures to 'clean up' their township, 24 June 1959. The townships where black workers and their families lived were separated from the towns where whites lived. They provided only basic accommodation and no security.

Indigenous people's rights

In North and South America, Australia and New Zealand, **indigenous people** (the original inhabitants) were thrown off their land when white settlers arrived. By the 20th century, most lived in poverty with no citizenship rights at all. In some Latin American countries, such as Guatemala, government troops attacked, tortured and sometimes murdered indigenous people. Indigenous women have campaigned for their people's rights to land, their culture and citizenship. In 1992, Rigoberta Menchú, a Guatemalan Mayan woman, was awarded the Nobel Peace Prize for her work defending indigenous people's rights.

In Australia until the 1960s, many Aboriginal children were taken away from their mothers without consent, to be raised in white families. This was an attempt to destroy Aboriginal culture and language. Across Australia, millions of women of all races and backgrounds have joined Women for Wik,(1997-2000) a huge campaign supporting Aboriginal rights.

Campaigning women

Many women have rejected the goals of male leaders and harsh and repressive governments, campaigning instead on **human rights** and environmental issues. All around the world, women have taken action to make their views heard, often devising imaginative and daring tactics to get their message across.

The 'Mothers of the Disappeared' in Argentina

In the 1970s, a brutal military regime ruled Argentina. Up to 20,000 people were kidnapped by soldiers and never seen again. Evidence eventually emerged showing that most had been tortured and then murdered. These people became known as the 'Disappeared'. Braving great danger, the 'Mothers of the Disappeared' protested against the brutal murders by walking silently round the central square of Buenos Aires, wearing white head scarves and carrying photographs of their children.

'Mothers of the Disappeared' weep during a protest against the torture and murder of thousands of people by the Argentine military government during the 1970s.

Women and the environment

Women have found peaceful new methods of campaigning on environmental issues, too. Often, especially in **developing countries**, women grow the food for their families, and so are particularly concerned about damage to the environment. In Uttar Pradesh in northern India, forest felling by commercial companies was causing frequent floods and landslides. Homes and livelihoods were threatened. In 1973, local women decided to organize protests to prevent any more trees from being felled. They marched out into the forest, and hugged the trees, protecting them with their own bodies to stop the felling.

Women for peace

Another popular movement in which women played an important role was the anti-nuclear campaign of the 1980s. Hundreds of thousands of women in Europe and North America protested against

Trees and human rights

Professor Wangari Mathaai, a Kenyan woman, is the founder of the environmental Green Belt Movement. Under her leadership, 50,000 women and school children planted more than 10 million trees in Kenya, improving the land and preventing soil erosion. In 1992 she was arrested and beaten for supporting human rights.

the build-up of nuclear weapons. They rejected their governments' military strategy of nuclear deterrence, or 'mutually assured destruction' (known for short as MAD), by which each **superpower** stockpiled enough nuclear weapons to destroy each other several times over, to deter the other side from starting war. Many protesters were women who had never been on demonstrations before, but they wanted to bring up their children in peace, without fear of nuclear war

Women set up peace camps outside American army and nuclear weapons bases in Europe, Australia and North America. In Britain in December 1982, 30,000 women linked arms around the Greenham Common American Air Force base, to protest at the deployment of nuclear cruise missiles. Eventually, American cruise missiles were removed from Europe as **Cold War** tensions subsided after the late 1980s.

Women across the divide

Some longstanding conflicts, such as those in Northern Ireland, and in Israel and Palestine, have affected women and their families for many generations. Yet despite the fear, violence and hatred that often characterizes such conflicts women have succeeded in working together to promote peace. They often focus on interests common to women from any background, rather than on the differences, religious or political, that divide them, for instance **domestic violence**, rape, childcare and conditions at work.

Guns or healthcare?

In 1986, Swedish anti-militarist campaigner Inga Thorsson compared health and military spending around the world: *'There is one soldier per 43 people but only one doctor for 1030 people. Every minute 30 children die from hunger and disease – but every minute the world spends $2 million for military purposes.'*

In 1997, Protestant and Catholic women formed the Women's Coalition in Northern Ireland. At the peace talks of 1997-98 they helped to bridge gaps between the main parties. In Israel, a movement called Coalition of Women for a Just Peace brings together Israeli and Palestinian women. They work to break down barriers between the two cultures, and to try and create a fair and lasting peace.

In 1997, Protestant and Catholic women formed the Women's Coalition in Northern Ireland, helping to bridge the gap between the main parties in peace talks. Here a woman holds a paper dove at a Belfast peace rally.

Women and human rights

Every man, woman and child has **human rights** – that is, the right to live without fear for their life or liberty. Human rights began to be defined after 1945. But statements and declarations of human rights are not always properly enforced, and there are many violations around the world. Violations of women's human rights are often specifically related to their sex, as these two pages show.

What are human rights?

In response to atrocities during World War II, human rights were set out in the **United Nations**' Universal Declaration of Human Rights in 1948. This charter, signed by governments all around the world, defines freedoms to which every human being is entitled, whatever their sex, race, language or religion. These freedoms include the rights to a fair trial and not to be tortured or unfairly imprisoned, rights to privacy, marriage and family life, political rights and rights of equality.

Women as refugees

Refugees are people who have been forced to flee their homes to escape violence and persecution. Often they are escaping from human rights violations – and they may be vulnerable to further violations as they seek a safe place to stay. Women and children make up more than half of the world's estimated twelve million refugees. Women are sometimes escaping persecution because of their sex, for instance to escape a forced marriage or female genital mutilation, and have often struggled to be accepted as refugees.

Rape as a war crime

In wars throughout history, soldiers have raped women of the opposing side. A horrific example was the organized campaign of rape of Bosnian women

Kurdish women refugees living in miserable conditions in a refugee camp in Turkey. Refugees must often rely on aid to feed and clothe their families, unable to work or grow food as they could at home.

by Serb soldiers, during the war in the former Yugoslavia in the 1990s. Eventually, some of the soldiers who had taken part were prosecuted and imprisoned by an international court at The Hague for human rights violations. This was the first time that rape had been successfully prosecuted as a war crime.

Contemporary slavery

Slavery was abolished in most countries in the 19th century – but new forms of slavery ensnare many thousands of girls and women around the world, denying them their human rights. Child labour is one form, with hundreds of thousands of girls (and boys, too) forced to work instead of going to school, for instance in West Africa harvesting the cocoa crops sold to make chocolate, or in parts of Asia making trainers for **multinational corporations**. In the Far East, many women and young girls are trapped by poverty in domestic slavery, or in the sex tourism trade, where some have contracted HIV, the virus that leads to AIDS.

Double discrimination

Women with disabilities, like women in other minority groups, may experience double **discrimination**. Girls and women with disabilities face discrimination because of their disability as well as their gender. In societies where girls receive less schooling than boys, girls with disabilities may find it even harder to get any education. Around the world, women and men with disabilities are organizing campaigns for equal rights.

Aung San Suu Kyi

In 1990, Aung San Suu Kyi led her party to victory in elections in Burma, ruled since 1962 by harsh military dictators. Despite this she has not been allowed to govern, living under **house arrest** since the elections. Each week, people gather outside her home, risking imprisonment to hear her speak. Her experience shows how human rights can be violated despite the UN Declaration of Human Rights and other international agreements, if they are not properly enforced.

Aung San Suu Kyi, who was democratically elected the leader of Burma in 1990. Despite international protests, the military dictatorship has violated her human rights, keeping her under house arrest and refusing to allow her to govern.

Education of girls and women

Throughout the 20th century, access to education came to be recognized as a basic **human right**. In 1958, the **United Nations** introduced its Convention against **Discrimination** in Education. Great improvements have been made in girls' and women's education in many countries – but there are still parts of the world where girls receive little or no schooling.

Educating wives and home-makers

Early in the 20th century, it was thought that education was wasted on girls, since they were destined only to become wives and mothers. As a result, girls, and especially working-class girls, were given only basic education, concentrating on home-making skills such as cooking, sewing and laundering. Girls were not taught other skills which would allow them to earn their own living and build a career.

Richer families could afford to pay for better schooling though the curriculum offered to these girls was often weak on science and mathematics. This meant that girls who did go on to university were already steered towards arts subjects.

A women's dissection class at Women's College Hospital, Philadelphia, USA in 1911. Around the world, women fought for many decades for the right to study for professions, such as medicine.

Chinese women's education

In 1924 the Chinese women's movement issued this proclamation:
'Let boys and girls receive the same instruction. Let all careers be open to girls. … Let the old educational system which produced "good wives and tender mothers" be abolished and one created which turns girls into real human beings.'

Women and higher education

For centuries, women were not allowed to study at universities. This meant that many careers and professions were closed to them. When women students were allowed to study at some universities or other higher education institutions they braved hostility and ridicule from male teachers and students.

THIS TABLE SHOWS WHEN WOMEN WERE FIRST ALLOWED TO STUDY AT UNIVERSITIES OR OTHER HIGHER EDUCATION INSTITUTIONS IN SOME COUNTRIES.

1833	USA	1908	GERMANY
1871	BRITAIN	1915	TURKEY
1871	NETHERLANDS	1925	ISRAEL
1877	INDIA	1964	JORDAN
1882	NORWAY		

Maria Montessori

Maria Montessori (1870-1952) grew up in Italy. After training as a doctor, she opened a school for children with learning difficulties. Unhappy with existing teaching methods, she devised her own. She believed that young children learned best through spontaneous play, taking responsibility for their own learning. These methods were found to work also with children without learning difficulties. Montessori methods have influenced mainstream teaching methods all around the world.

Girls' grades... and boys'

During the 1970s and 80s, there was concern in the **West** that girls were achieving lower grades than boys in traditionally male subjects, such as science and mathematics.

Teachers and educationalists worked hard to find ways of making these subjects more accessible to girls, building girls' confidence and improving their grades. However, in the last decade of the 20th century, the tables began to turn. Boys' exam results slipped behind girls' in many subjects, even in some traditionally male ones. Now educationalists are looking at ways to bring boys' grades back up again to match girls'.

Women learning to read and write in a Kenyan village. When women and girls are educated, they go on to have fewer and healthier children – an important strategy for improving life in developing countries.

Women and literacy

Despite real progress in tackling illiteracy over the last quarter of the 20th century, by 2000 there were still an estimated 900 million illiterate adults around the world, people who have never learned to read and write in their own language. Two-thirds, 600 million, are women. In **developing countries** all round the world, girls frequently get less schooling than boys. Girls are often expected to work at home or in the fields instead.

Research shows that where girls and women are educated, the birth rate falls and they have fewer and healthier children. Encouraging families to send their daughters to school and improving women's **literacy** are two essential strategies for improving life in many developing countries.

Domestic life

Women doing the washing in the backyard in the 1930s. This task meant fetching the water, heating it on a fire or stove, scrubbing clothing and sheets by hand, and then rinsing them and passing them through the mangle.

At the beginning of the 20th century, women were mainly responsible for childcare, as well as household tasks such as cooking, cleaning and laundry. During the century, new electrical machines such as fridges, vacuum cleaners and washing machines transformed many of these tasks. But recent research shows that even today, women still do most of the housework.

Men's work, women's work

Men are traditionally seen as the breadwinners, bringing in money by doing a paid job outside the home. In contrast, women's work in the home remains unpaid and rarely acknowledged. And yet, without this unpaid domestic work, the wage-earning economy would grind to a halt; on normal earnings, most men could not afford to pay a housekeeper, cook and nanny to replace the work done by their wives.

Heavy labour at home

In the **West** in 1900, without electricity or even running water in the house, women's domestic tasks such as laundry were hard, physical toil. Water had to be fetched and heated for washing and cooking. In addition, coal had to be carried, grates cleared and fires lit each day. Without fridges and freezers to preserve food, and no convenient ready-prepared meals, food had to be bought and cooked fresh each day.

Epitaph for a Tired Housewife

This traditional English rhyme in the style of a gravestone epitaph reflects the endless drudgery of women's housework before the introduction of labour-saving devices.

Here lies a poor woman who always was tired.
She lived in a house where help was not hired.
Her last words on earth were, 'Dear friends, I am going
Where washing ain't done, nor sweeping nor sewing;
But everything there is exact to my wishes,
For where they don't eat there's no washing of dishes.
Don't mourn for me now, don't mourn for me never;
I'm going to do nothing for ever and ever.'

Labour-saving devices

In the USA, Britain and other Western countries, electricity began to be installed in homes from the beginning of the century for the very wealthy, and through the 1920s to 1940s for most people. Labour-saving devices, such as washing machines and vacuum cleaners, made the work easier, though only the rich could afford them at first.

Today in the West most households have these machines, which have reduced the hard labour involved in housework, but they have not necessarily reduced the amount of time spent on it, since standards of cleanliness have risen as a result. Many people now expect to wear clean clothes most days, which was not the case before washing machines were widely available. In **developing countries**, meanwhile, most women must still do chores such as laundry by hand.

The new domestic servants?

After World War I, only the very richest families continued to employ **domestic servants**. But towards the end of the 20th century in the West, there was a rise in the number of people – usually women – employed to do domestic work in other people's homes. As more women went out to work, ordinary middle-class families started to pay people to work as cleaners, nannies or au pairs. As with domestic service in the early part of the century, this kind of work was often lonely and badly paid. Thousands of women from developing countries, such as Malaysia and Thailand, the Philippines and Latin America came as **migrant** workers to these jobs, sending their wages back home to support their families.

A house unkept

Women were judged by their housekeeping standards. There were some dissenting voices, though. In 1923, novelist Rose Macaulay told her readers, 'Let the house go unkept. Let it go to the devil, and see what happens. At the worst, a house unkept cannot be so distressing as a life unlived.'

Children in a nursery on a kibbutz (a co-operatively run community) in Israel. Many kibbutzim (kibbutz dwellers) organize shared cooking and childcare to free women from the burden and isolation of domestic work.

Marriage, motherhood and divorce

At the beginning of the 20th century, marriage for most women meant shifting from their father's control to their husband's, with the possibilty of decades of pregnancies and child rearing. While many women considered that their role as a mother was very important, not only to themselves, but to society in general, they argued that it did not receive the recognition and status it deserved. Throughout the 20th century, women fought for access to **contraception**, to enable them to manage the planning of their families, and for rights in marriage and on **divorce**.

Birth control

Contraceptives, or **birth control**, allow people to plan if or when they have children. Without birth control, a woman might have up to twenty children, damaging her health and forcing her to spend most of her life caring for her family. Often poor families could not afford to care for so many children.

Margaret Sanger set up the first birth-control clinic in 1916 in New York, USA. Queues formed outside. Sanger was arrested for breaking laws which restricted the distribution of contraceptives or information about them, but she won her case and went on to open 300 birth-control clinics. In Britain, despite protests from doctors and Christian groups, Marie Stopes opened a birth-control clinic in London in 1921.

In **developing countries** with poor healthcare, many women continue to have large families because many children die from malnutrition and disease. With no **pensions** or **welfare system**, it is the children who must provide for their parents in old age. Until parents can be fairly sure that their children will survive, many will be reluctant to use birth control. Furthermore some Catholic and Islamic leaders discourage birth control for religious reasons.

Motherhood by the book

Throughout the 20th century, women have been bombarded with advice from experts (often male) on how to raise children. Ideas have shifted from rigid, frosty

Margaret Sanger, American birth control pioneer, with her supporters outside the court in New York.

discipline to the more affectionate and relaxed approach recommended by Dr Benjamin Spock, Penelope Leach and others. In the 1950s and 60s, mothers who went out to work were accused of harming their children, although working fathers were never criticized. By the end of the 20th century many women in the **West** were working full-time, though in some countries part-time work had become a popular option, allowing mothers to earn money while still spending time with their children. Employment rights for working mothers have improved in the West, including maternity pay and the right to return to work after having children.

Women's property rights

Historically, when a woman married, everything she owned was transferred from her father's control to her husband's, as women were not allowed to own property, money or goods in their own right. Gradually through the late 19th and 20th centuries, Western countries changed their laws to give women equal property rights. However, in many developing countries, a husband still controls his wife's property.

Divorce

For centuries, divorce was difficult or illegal, even for women in the most unhappy, violent or abusive marriages. Through the 19th and 20th centuries, divorce has gradually been introduced in most countries around the world, despite disapproval from some religious leaders. Divorce is rising. This is partly due to legislation introduced in the 1960s that has made divorce easier for both men and women and partly because of women's growing economic **independence**. Divorce courts try to divide a couple's money fairly, but still many divorced women end up poorer than before. This is because few women can earn as much as their husband, especially if they have responsibility for the children.

In some cultures divorce is legally available, but in practice may not be a safe option for women. In some Islamic countries, for example, there is great pressure on women to maintain the family honour. Women accused of bringing shame on the family by filing for divorce or by having sex outside marriage can be severely punished by family members.

*A Hindu wedding ceremony in India, where the bride's family is expected to pay a **dowry** to the husband's family. Some wives have been killed because their dowry is too small. Women in India are campaigning for an end to dowries and the violence they can bring.*

23

Changes since 1960

Women's rights came to the fore again in the **West** in the 1960s, a time of fresh ideas and new sexual freedom among young people. A new women's political movement called 'Women's Liberation' questioned the role and status of women. Their campaigns shaped women's rights throughout the rest of the 20th century.

Women's Liberation movement

In the 1960s in the West, young women flocked to study as universities expanded. But women's job opportunities and earnings were still limited. Most women worked in low-paid clerical or service jobs. When they married, they were expected to stay at home and raise children.

In 1966, women in the USA, influenced by the **civil rights** movement of that time, set up the National Organization of Women (NOW). Women's Liberation groups sprang up and their ideas spread quickly in many countries, rich and poor.

Like the **suffragists**, the Women's Liberation movement campaigned for equal pay and equal rights at work, but they were also fighting for equality in relationships – summed up in their slogan, 'the personal is political'. By this they meant that the personal relationships within an individual marriage or family are part of a wider political framework, where men have more power than women.

A woman's right to choose

Women's Liberation fought for a woman's right to decide for herself about her own life and her body – rather than her husband, family, employer, the government or church deciding for her. Campaigners set up refuges or safe houses for women fleeing from violent husbands. Two other important developments were the **contraceptive** pill and access to **abortion**.

Available from the 1960s, the contraceptive pill allowed women to have sex without fear of getting

Demonstrators from the National Women's Liberation Movement protesting at the Miss America Pageant in Atlantic City, 1968. As part of this protest demonstrators crowned a sheep. Feminists found such beauty contests degrading and felt they encouraged men to judge only women's sexual attractiveness.

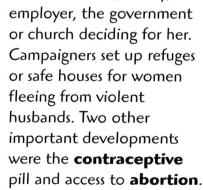

pregnant. At first, it was available to married women only. In Britain, the Marie Stopes Clinic held its first sessions for unmarried women in secret because many people disapproved. The pill allowed the sexual freedom at the heart of 1960s youth culture. But some feared that young women would come under pressure from men to have sex without being able to say no.

Abortion

Abortion, or termination of pregnancy, was banned in most countries until the 1960s. Sometimes pregnant women were forced to seek out an illegal abortion if they could not support a child because of poverty or ill-health, or because of feelings of shame if they were young or unmarried. Many women died or became infertile as a result of unsafe illegal abortions.

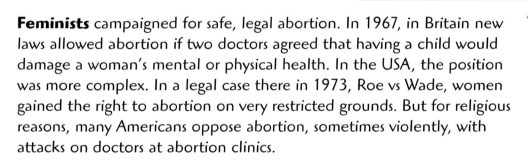

Feminists campaigned for safe, legal abortion. In 1967, in Britain new laws allowed abortion if two doctors agreed that having a child would damage a woman's mental or physical health. In the USA, the position was more complex. In a legal case there in 1973, Roe vs Wade, women gained the right to abortion on very restricted grounds. But for religious reasons, many Americans oppose abortion, sometimes violently, with attacks on doctors at abortion clinics.

Shaping the future

In the USA, feminists and other campaigners fought hard to change the US constitution with the Equal Rights Amendment (ERA), which would have guaranteed equal treatment in all areas of life. Although it was accepted by Congress in 1972, the ERA never became law, because several states refused to ratify it. The US constitution remains without an Equal Rights Amendment. This was a major blow for women's rights in the USA.

The Women's Liberation movement was fairly shortlived, and it remained a largely white and middle-class movement. Even so, many of the movement's aims were fulfilled, in the West at least. In the European Community, legislation now outlaws unequal treatment of women. Young women today expect freedom and equality as a matter of course.

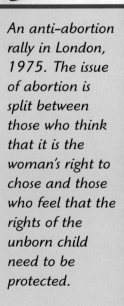

An anti-abortion rally in London, 1975. The issue of abortion is split between those who think that it is the woman's right to chose and those who feel that the rights of the unborn child need to be protected.

Healthcare and medicine

Women are the main users of healthcare services, giving birth, looking after their families' health and living longer than men. Healthcare and medicine developed rapidly through the 20th century, bringing huge improvements in women's and men's health. However many **developing countries** are too poor for their people to benefit from medical advances, and women's health is especially badly affected as a result.

New health services

In 1900, without free healthcare, women – and especially poor women – were particularly at risk. Their health was weakened by frequent pregnancies, and many died in childbirth, in dirty or dangerous surroundings, often without the skilled help of a trained **midwife**.

In Britain and much of Europe after World War II, national health services were set up or extended, offering free healthcare to all. For millions of women, this meant that at last they could get proper care during pregnancy and in childbirth. In recent years many women's lives have been saved by preventative healthcare such as screening for the early symptoms of cervical and breast cancer. In the USA, where healthcare is based on private insurance, many poor women still get inadequate medical care.

Women's psychological health?

The last quarter of the 20th century brought new concerns over women's psychological health in the **West**. Here women are constantly bombarded with media images and glossy advertising showing an ideal body shape – much thinner than most women's natural shape. The multi-million dollar slimming industry encourages women to buy low-fat and dieting products.

These pressures have led to a steep rise in **anorexia** and other eating disorders among girls and young women. Sometimes these are so extreme that they lead to hospitalization and even death. At the same time, there is growing demand for expensive plastic surgery to change

Children orphaned by the AIDS virus in Nairobi, Kenya. The children are protesting against pharmaceutical companies who charge unaffordable prices for drugs which might have saved their parents' lives.

women's body shapes, such as breast enlargement or reduction and tummy tucks as well as facial alteration – all in the quest for female physical perfection. This is in stark contrast to some of the less developed countries of the world where the main concerns are hunger, **malnutrition**, disease and high **infant mortality**.

Women's health in developing countries

Poor people in developing countries still live in unhealthy conditions, often without sanitation or clean drinking water, and without access to doctors, nurses or healthcare. In some very poor areas, such as parts of Bangladesh, as few as five per cent of women giving birth are attended by a trained midwife or doctor (compared with 98–100 per cent in the West). A woman in Africa is 200 times more likely to die from a pregnancy-related complication than a woman in the West.

Women with HIV and AIDS

By the end of 2000, over 16 million women had HIV or AIDS, over 80 per cent of them in the developing world. In the affluent West, drugs are used to slow down the progress of the disease. People with AIDS can now expect to live for many years, but in poorer parts of the world, governments cannot afford the drug manufacturers' high prices, and so people are left to die.

Reproductive technology

From the 1970s onwards reproductive technology used new scientific methods to overcome infertility, bringing great joy to some women who would otherwise have been unable to have babies. However, treatment is very expensive (and often unsuccessful), and most health authorities will not pay for it, seeing curing disease as more important.

Reproductive technology is developing very quickly, raising many complex ethical issues. Now that tests can show the sex of an embryo in the womb, female embryos are sometimes aborted because parents want a son instead. In addition, some parents leave their baby girls to die because they want a boy. This has led to a serious population imbalance in countries such as Pakistan and China, with tens of millions of 'missing females'.

*Louise Brown, the world's first test-tube baby, born in 1978. She was conceived by **in vitro fertilization**. Here her parents talk on American television about the events leading to her birth.*

27

Women and work 1900–39

At the beginning of the 20th century, while most rich women stayed at home, working-class women worked long hours for very low pay. Women were excluded from many jobs by their limited education or by employers' expectations. For instance very few women were able to train and work as doctors or other professionals. World War I however, was to bring radical changes to women's work.

Women as workers

In 1900, working-class women worked to help make ends meet for their families, often in backbreaking or hazardous jobs. They were paid less than men, and they could rarely join **trade unions** to press for better rights and pay. In cities women worked in **sweatshops**, places that demanded the most work for the lowest pay. In rural and coastal areas they might work in the fields or in the fishing industry. Millions of women toiled for hours every day as **domestic servants**.

Women in World War I

In 1914 war broke out and governments all over Europe soon began to encourage women to take over jobs left empty by men who had gone to fight. Women worked in public transport, police forces, munitions factories and in the fields. In Germany by 1917, there were over 700,000 women working in heavy industry – six times as many as in 1913.

German window cleaners on their way to work in 1905. Working-class women did many types of heavy work.

War work for many women meant twelve-hour shifts, seven days a week – and they were still paid far less than men had been for the same work. But old prejudices were challenged as women coped well with men's jobs.

Some women travelled to the front, where the fighting was taking place, to serve as nurses and ambulance drivers. A few took on daring roles as spies and resistance fighters behind enemy lines, including Edith Cavell, a British nurse who helped prisoners to escape, and a Dutch dancer known as Mata Hari who worked as a German spy. Both were executed when they fell into enemy hands.

After the War

Women, especially those who were married, were expected to leave men's jobs free for the soldiers returning from the front. But the world was changing. Many women were reluctant to give up their new-found **independence**, and were prepared to explore new types of work to earn a living. Domestic service was growing increasingly unpopular. All over America and Europe, women took jobs in factories, mostly unskilled and low-paid, where new mass-production methods were used to make all kinds of goods from cars to shoes to typewriters. Office work and shop work held out a better future for many aspiring young women from the lower middle classes.

Rather than starve in the drought-ridden American Dustbowl states in the 1930s, women and their families abandoned their farms and travelled in great hardship to California in search of work. Photographer Dorothea Lange, who took this picture, documented their desperate plight.

Depression and the New Deal

From 1929, the **Great Depression** rippled around the world. Unemployment soared, reaching 30 per cent of the workforce in Australia, Norway and Germany. Many women were badly affected by poverty and hunger, especially those who needed to earn money to support themselves and their families. In the USA, President Roosevelt set up the New Deal, creating public service jobs building dams and other huge projects to get people back into work. But only a few schemes for women were set up.

Paid holidays

Most workers did not get paid holidays until the 1930s. A French woman remembers,
'You have no idea what a tremendous joy it was to get paid holidays. The whole of Paris, all the workshops, all the factories, everywhere people went crazy.'

The Dustbowl

For rural women on small farms all around the world, life was gruelling and often lonely. They lived, worked and raised families in poor conditions, often in homes without electricity or toilets. On the American Great Plains in 1933, massive dust storms whipped away the thin topsoil, loosened by lack of rain and decades of over-ploughing. On thousands of small family farms, it was impossible to grow food or cotton crops and families starved.

Women's service in World War II

Women played an even more active role in World War II than they had in World War I. Once again, governments needed women to take on men's jobs at home. This time, war work brought important changes in women's employment, including part-time work, childcare and demands for equal pay.

Women on active service

In the face of the disapproval of some senior officers, in both the UK and the USA, women's auxiliary units were set up in the army, navy and air force. Women pilots, including famous names such as Amy Johnson, were eventually allowed to fly military planes. They were set to work ferrying planes to where they were needed. Women trained for technical tasks, such as guiding pilots by radio, and operating radar and anti-aircraft searchlights. General Eisenhower, supreme commander in the allied invasion of Germany and future president of the USA, was a strong supporter of women in active roles behind the lines.

Women pilots of the British Air Transport Auxiliary Service, who ferried planes from factories to airports during World War II.

> ### A war-work organizer remembers:
> 'I remember three girls from Bootle [Lancashire]. They were marvellous. They became the most efficient tractor drivers, and got used to humping sacks of potatoes. I can't think of anything they couldn't do.'

War work at home

Right across Europe, women worked in munitions factories to support their country's war effort. In Britain in 1941 women under 40 were **conscripted** for war work in the factories, fields or other essential jobs. In the USA there was no conscription, but **propaganda** campaigns, encouraged women to support the war effort. A lasting image from this era is 'Rosie the Riveter', painted by Norman Rockwell, and featured on the front cover of the *Saturday Evening Post*, 29 May 1943. Rosie looked strong and capable of anything. Such propaganda was successful in persuading women to train as welders, electricians and shipfitters.

Equal rights at work?

But even in war work, sexual and racial **discrimination** was widespread. Some male supervisors were reluctant to believe that women could do technical work as well as men, although they were soon proved wrong. Women were paid less than men for the same jobs. In the USA, African-American women were often directed to badly paid jobs, for instance kitchen work, until protest marches got them into higher paid manufacturing work. Many more women joined **trade unions** to demand equal pay.

A US poster showing Rosie the Riveter, painted by Norman Rockwell. Propaganda like this encouraged American women to lend their muscle to the war effort.

There were other changes too. Part-time work was introduced to fit around women's responsibilities at home. More women worked as dentists, lawyers, architects and in other professions. Women photographers, like Margaret Bourke-White and Lee Miller, and journalists such as Martha Gellhorn and Iris Morley, recorded the horrors of war. Iris Morley was one of the first British correspondents to send news of the Nazi concentration camps in 1945.

Childcare for women war workers

British propaganda posters were published to encourage people to look after war workers' children.
'If you can't go to the factory, help the neighbour who can.
Caring for war workers' children is a national service.
Arrange now with a neighbour to look after her children when she goes to her war work.'

Childcare to help working mothers

In peacetime, childcare for working mothers was not a government priority. But when women's labour was needed for the war effort, the British government set up hundreds of nurseries to look after children, allowing mothers to go out to work. In the USA, most working mothers still had to make their own arrangements for childcare while they worked.

31

Women's work in the post-war era

By the end of World War II in 1945, Europe was devastated. With millions of men killed or missing, it was often the women who started rebuilding. From the late 1950s the **West** enjoyed decades of confidence and prosperity. But there were hard times for women in other parts of the world.

Back to the kitchen

When peace came, just as after World War I, women in the West were expected to leave their jobs for the returning men. Having experienced a few years of financial **independence** many women found this disappointing and frustrating.

The United States had grown stronger through the war. Europe and Japan worked hard to rebuild shattered industries. By the mid-1950s, living standards in the West and Japan had risen to higher levels than before the war. Peace and optimism brought a 'baby boom'. Even though there were no longer legal restrictions on married women working, as there had been in pre-war Britain, women and especially mothers were encouraged to stay at home. Their work was seen as bringing up the children and keeping a spotless home. Middle-class women who did work were mainly confined to traditionally female jobs, such as teaching, nursing or secretarial work. Working-class women often did shifts in factories that were specially made to fit childcare responsibilities or they worked in shops, in catering or did cleaning work.

Russian women resurfacing the roads in Moscow, a job usually seen in the West as men's work.

Trade union struggles

Women were still paid less than men for doing the same or equivalent jobs. In 1965, women's earnings in the USA were still only 60 per cent of men's earnings. Many women, including badly paid African-American, Asian and Hispanic women, joined **trade unions** to fight against **discrimination** at work. Strikes by women, such as health workers in New York, and sewing machinists in 1968, which brought Ford's UK car factory at Dagenham to a standstill, showed that their work was as important as men's. Gradually, these struggles brought about some improvement in women's rights at work.

British workers on strike for better rights at work in the 1970s. Many black and Asian women took their struggle for equal rights through the trade unions.

Sexual harassment flourished in the male culture of many workplaces, restricting women's careers and making their working lives miserable. In the UK, in 1983, after pressure from women members, the Trade Union Congress produced guidelines to crack down on this problem.

Women in the Communist world

In the Soviet Union, so many men had been killed in the war that many women remained unmarried, or brought up children on their own. Western ideas about traditional male and female roles did not apply in the **Communist** world, where women worked as engineers, doctors, machinists and labourers. Women were expected to work long hours in the factories on the same terms as men.

However many Communist economies failed to provide ordinary goods such as washing machines or even sanitary towels to improve women's day-to-day lives. There were frequent food shortages, and women had to queue at food shops every day to buy enough to feed their families.

Women's work in developing countries

Women were badly affected by changes in **developing countries**. In the 1960s and 70s, rich nations sent aid in the form of loans to help developing countries build up their industry. But as interest rates rose the cost of paying back the loans rose steeply. Many poor countries were forced to cut services such as health and education. This hit women especially hard, as they needed medical care in childbirth and were often responsible for bringing up their children. Unemployment, poverty and hunger grew rapidly.

Women's work at the end of the century

'Equal pay for equal work', a central plank of the Women's Liberation campaigns of the 1970s, has not yet been achieved everywhere. But by the end of the 20th century, women were free to choose a far wider range of jobs, including manual and professional roles which had always been seen as men's work.

Equal pay?

By 2000, women's earnings in the USA and Britain were hovering at around 75 per cent, just three-quarters the rate of men's earnings. But this figure masked wide variations; for instance, Hispanic women in the USA earned just 48 cents for every dollar earned by a man.

A US female soldier takes a break during training exercises in Saudi Arabia.

Childcare for working mothers

While women without children were finding more and more work opportunities opening up to them, women with children still faced many barriers. Employers were often reluctant to take on women with children, fearing a clash in responsibilities of work and family. Reliable and affordable childcare for those that wanted to return to work was the only solution to this problem.

Scandinavia led the way, providing plenty of high quality childcare for mothers who went out to work. But in other countries, childcare was expensive and in short supply. Many women were still forced to rely on precarious arrangements with relatives, friends and neighbours to look after their children after school and during holidays.

Women into traditionally male jobs

Women fought for the right to work in many different fields traditionally reserved for men. For example, in 1992 the Church of England began to ordain women priests, following more progressive American and British churches and synagogues, which had allowed women priests and rabbis since the 1970s. By the end of the 20th century, women could serve as soldiers in the front line along with men in the UK, Germany, the USA and other countries.

Through the 20th century, girls and women gradually overcame male scepticism and resistance to work as scientists. Even then, they often had to fight for recognition, as male colleagues took credit for their work.

Globalization: women in developing countries ...

In the 1980s and 90s, **multinational corporations** started to transfer their manufacturing from the **West** to factories in Asia and Latin America. There they could pay workers (often women) much lower wages than in the West. This is part of a process called **globalization**. In countries such as in China, Malaysia and Mexico, young women worked in multinationals' factories, manufacturing electronic equipment, textiles and footwear. Many worked up to eighteen hours a day in conditions often harmful to their health. Fortunately **trade unions** as well as campaigning groups, such as Oxfam, put pressure on multinationals to improve working conditions in their factories.

A young woman at work in an electronics factory in China, 1987. As part of the process known as globalization, large multinational corporations have located their factories in countries where pay and working conditions are lower than in the West.

...and in the West

As a result of globalization, many factories closed down across Europe and the USA. Millions of jobs traditionally done by men were lost. In many industrial cities, new work patterns emerged. Part-time jobs in service industries, such as catering – mainly filled by women – replaced men's jobs in manufacturing.

Women in business

Women often found it more difficult than men to set up their own businesses because money lenders were often sceptical about whether women had the necessary skills for this sort of work. One example is Anita Roddick. She had great difficulty persuading any bank to lend her money to start manufacturing and opening shops to sell her goods. Despite this her cosmetic business, Body Shop, became very successful. Other successful business women include fashion designer Vivienne Westwood and television presenter Oprah Winfrey, who has gone on to manage her own television company.

Entertainment, media and the arts

Throughout history, women have worked as actors, singers and entertainers, though they have had to fight for equal pay. But in many other art forms, women have had to challenge prejudice to be taken seriously – and to get funding for their work. Often they have struggled to carve out time from their domestic responsibilities for their art. Women have fought for a more influential role in the new media that developed throughout the 20th century, from radio and cinema to television and information technology.

Craft or art?

Women's traditional creative skills in needlework have been downgraded as craft, rather than as higher-status art. Even at the radical German Bauhaus, college of architecture and design, set up in 1919, women were expected to work only in textiles. They had to fight to take part in other art forms, such as painting or architecture.

Women in film, theatre and television

In the first half of the 20th century, going to the movies was hugely popular. A British study in 1937 found some women and girls went twelve times a week. Glamorous Hollywood women filmstars were models of feminine style – and often grew very rich.

However, women who wanted to direct their own films had a struggle to raise funds and very few succeeded in becoming filmmakers. In the theatre, the situation was better and more women directors found success, such as Jude Kelly and Abigail Morris in the UK.

The single most important mass-medium of the 20th century was television, and women's profile as journalists, directors and presenters grew towards the end of the century. Though news agendas were still largely dictated by male interests, with an emphasis on party politics, war, disaster and male sports, a few women journalists reported from war zones around the world. Individual women also had immense influence via television. For instance in the USA, Oprah Winfrey shaped the reading habits of millions with her monthly television bookclub.

Oprah Winfrey, successful actress, chat show host and business woman, interviews presidential candidate Al Gore on her television programme in September 2000.

Women writers

Historically women writers had an uphill battle to get their work published and often they resorted to adopting a male name in order to do so. As the 20th century progressed more and more women's writing found its way into print and particularly from the 1970s onwards, women's writing flourished, promoted by both **feminist** and mainstream publishers. In the US, women such as Toni Morrison and Maya Angelou, were writing from a female African-American perspective – their books winning much popular acclaim.

Women musicians

Women musicians have often struggled to make a living from their work. In the segregated southern states of the USA, African-American musicians were rarely allowed to perform for white audiences. In the 1920s, African-American jazz singer Josephine Baker worked instead in more easy-going France, where she became a star. In the 1960s, African-American women's groups such as the Supremes achieved great popularity – but often their recording contracts meant that they kept little of the money their success earned. By the end of the 20th century this situation had changed and there are many examples of very successful women, like the Spice Girls and Madonna, earning large fortunes through popular music.

Female composers, like female artists, have had to struggle to get their work in front of an audience. American composer Ruth Schonthal reflected upon the experience of women artists in many fields when she said, 'It has been a tremendous struggle to find time and energy to compose.' Without the recognition and funding that support many male composers, she earned her living by teaching and playing in clubs.

Evelyn Glennie, world renowned percussionist with a hearing disability. Most orchestras have abandoned their men-only traditions, employing women musicians on equal terms, except for the Vienna Philharmonic Orchestra, which still bans women.

Funny women

Female comedians were a relative rarity until late in the 20th century – women were expected to be beautiful, but not funny. American singer and comic Bette Midler was an exception, starring in cabaret and movies from the late 1960s. From the 1980s, women comedians started to break into television sitcoms and stand-up comedy. Many of their jokes were at men's expense, getting their own back after centuries of male sexist humour!

Fashion statements

Coco Chanel (left), a French fashion designer working in Paris, designed stylish, loose-fitting clothes made of soft, comfortable fabrics. Many women welcomed these relaxed new fashions.

Women's clothing is an indicator of sexual politics – with fashion items such as corsets and high heels often cramping women's freedom of movement. From long skirts in 1900 to power-dressing trouser suits in 2000, sweeping changes in **Western** women's fashions mirrored some of the changes in women's lives.

Health and wealth

In 1900, Western women wore full-length skirts for modesty, with tight-laced corsets to pinch their waists – often restricting their breathing and damaging their health. Rich women displayed their wealth by wearing elaborate, opulent gowns. Meanwhile, poor women might own only one dress, which would be mended again and again.

New Woman, new look

Fashion began to change early in the 20th century, so-called 'New Women' began to challenge some of the traditional expectations of how women should dress. Some took to wearing trousers or knickerbockers, which allowed them more freedom of movement. Skirt hemlines rose, though not yet above the knee.

After World War I, women started to abandon their corsets and some of the old restrictive fashions. Coco Chanel, a French designer working in Paris, designed loose-fitting fashions made of soft, comfortable fabrics. The 'flappers', fashionable young women of the 1920s, danced in revealing dresses that seemed shocking at the time.

Wartime austerity

During both world wars, new clothes were a rare luxury. In Britain, fabric was rationed along with food and furniture. Governments encouraged fashions which required less fabric – for instance shorter, narrow skirts. Then, when peace came, women enjoyed new and freer fashions again.

The shock of the young

Young women's fashions in the second half of the 20th century often seemed outrageous to older generations. Women's clothes in the 1960s reflected the sexual freedom of the times. Hemlines rose and rose – until the 'mini skirt' couldn't get any shorter. **Androgynous** styles, suitable for both sexes, reduced the difference between women's and men's clothing among hippies in the 1960s, and again in the late 1970s when punk rock spread from Britain around the world. Young punk rockers rejected their parents' values, dressing in black binliners and ripped clothing held together with safety pins. Women and men alike wore garish makeup and spiky hairstyles supported by masses of hairspray.

East, west, best dressed?

Western designers have often borrowed fashion ideas from around the world, from Indian prints to African textiles. But Western fashions influenced people in other cultures, too, often weakening distinctive local styles and traditions.

'No Logo'

Throughout the developed world, fashion has been dominated by heavily-advertised brands such as Nike or Gap. Branded clothing and trainers are sold at very high prices, despite being cheaply manufactured in **developing countries** by poorly-paid workers – mainly women and children. This increases the manufacturers' profits.

Naomi Klein, a young Canadian woman, is one of the leaders of the 'No Logo' movement. This movement protests against such profiteering, which cheats both the workers and the consumers. Instead, supporters campaign for better working conditions for people making clothes, shoes and other goods.

Clothing at school

Many girls are forced to wear a skirt as part of their school uniform. Some girls have argued that this **discriminates** against them as it is impractical and uncomfortable in cold weather. Individual girls have challenged school rules, taking their cases to court. Recent court rulings have decided that it is unfair for schools to impose different rules for girls and boys.

This French girl is protesting against the ban on wearing the Islamic veil at school. In France it is argued that schools should be **secular**, not religious, establishments. In 1994, some Islamic girls went on hunger strike, forced to choose between their faith and their education.

Sport

In 1900, women were expected to take part only in 'ladylike' sports. Athleticism and competition were thought likely to 'de-sex' them. Throughout the 20th century, women fought to take part in all sports, and with equal rewards for winning.

'Ladies sports'

Traditional ladies' sports were restricted to tennis, badminton, croquet and golf, together with dancing, riding and skating. In women's long, restrictive clothing, most other sports were impractical. In addition, there was concern that too much physical exercise might damage women's delicate health and their ability to have children.

New freedoms

The 1920s saw a break away from these concerns. Isadora Duncan's free-expression dancing increased the popularity of exercise through movement to music. Ballet became increasingly popular, too, and many dance schools opened.

In 1994, Liv Arnesen of Sweden became the first woman to ski alone to the South Pole.

In 1926, nineteen-year-old Gertrude Ederle broke both male and female records when she swam the English Channel in just fourteen and a half hours – challenging sceptics who thought that women could not compete athletically with men. Other 1920s record breakers included golfer Glenn Collate and Floret McCrutcheon, who defeated the reigning male champion Jimmy Smith, in 1927, in the sport of bowls.

Commercial organizers began to see that women could be crowd-pullers in sport. The skimpy fashions of the 1920s narrowed the gap between sport and glamour, as women tennis players and other sportswomen started to wear more revealing, fashionable clothes. Women athletes have continued to struggle to find a balance between muscular fitness and femininity.

The Olympic Games

Women were barred from the modern Olympic Games until 1920, when they were allowed to compete in a very limited range of sports. In reaction, the Women's Olympic Games were held between 1922 and 1934, attracting competitors and spectators from all over the world. Steadily the proportion of women taking part in the Olympics rose, reaching 38 per cent in 2000, with some national teams, including Norway, China and the Democratic Republic of the Congo, with over 50 per cent women. Equestrian events are the only sports where women and men compete together.

Untraditional sports

In the 1970s, women began to take up traditionally unfeminine sports. For instance, by 1976 there were 10,000 women weightlifters in the USA. Instead of dancing on the sidelines as cheerleaders, girls started to take up traditionally male sports – often against strong opposition. In 1974, ten-year-old Frances Pescatore was not allowed to play baseball in a Little League team in New Jersey, USA. She challenged this discrimination, and won the right to play along with the boys.

Girls' and womens' football teams are now popular, and women's cricket tournaments are held in cricketing countries all around the world. Today women compete in shot putting, wrestling and even boxing.

Britain's Tanni Grey–Thompson, one of the women athletes competing at the Paralympic Games, which take place straight after the Olympic Games. There is increasing worldwide interest, sponsorship and television coverage of the Paralympic Games.

Equal prize money

Sports competition organizers had always paid women lower prize money than men. In 1970, top women tennis players including Billie-Jean King, Rosemary Casals and Ann Jones protested by simply refusing to play. The organizers soon had to give way. Women drew in massive audiences, and there was no justification for smaller prizes. A BBC commentator conceded that they had proved their worth 'game, set and match'. But this battle has had to be fought again and again in many sports.

Women's rights into the 21st century

By the end of the 20th century, many women had achieved many more rights than their great-grandmothers had a hundred years earlier. But there is still much work to be done to win equal rights for all the world's women in the 21st century and beyond.

Girls and women succeeding?

Girls are achieving well at school, and in the **West** at least, women go on to study at university in similar numbers to men. At work, too, women are developing their careers and moving into senior posts. Equal pay for equal work is accepted in principle, and many countries now have maternity benefits to make sure that women can take time off to have a family and then resume their career.

However, the proportion of women in the very top jobs, such as managing director, is still small. Many women reach an invisible barrier, known as the 'glass ceiling', which prevents them from achieving these most senior positions, especially in the private sector. Sex **segregation** is still common in the workplace, with women concentrated in lower-paid work such as catering and childcare.

The double burden

For many couples where both partners work full-time, women find that they are still doing most or all of the shopping, cooking and cleaning – the so-called 'double burden'. Women still spend more time than men looking after their children, as well as caring for elderly relatives. Studies have shown that these tasks leave women with less leisure time than men.

This woman has bought a rickshaw with a loan from the Grameen Bank in Bangladesh. This bank lends small amounts of money to women so that they can start businesses, often bringing their families out of generations of poverty.

Women and poverty

In the West, welfare provision put an end to hunger and malnutrition. But according to the **United Nations**, by 1995 about a quarter of the world's population was still living in extreme poverty in **developing countries**, on an income of less than one US dollar each day. Of these, nearly three-quarters were women and girls – who get less education and training to gain the skills needed to get out of poverty.

Many developing countries were also burdened with the problem of repaying the interest on loans made to them by more wealthy nations. This often resulted in them having to divert money away from welfare, health and education services. Campaigners for Jubilee 2000, (now renamed Drop the Debt), argue that the rich West should no longer demand these enormous interest payments. Britain and other governments in the West have at last made a start on this process. In 1999 they promised to cancel debts totalling $100 billion, although less than $12 billion had actually been written off by the end of the century.

Gains and losses

Women's campaigns achieved improved rights in many countries around the world. But in some areas, women's rights are decreasing. In Afghanistan and other countries with **fundamentalist** regimes, women are no longer allowed to study or to go out to work. Many Islamic women have argued that true Islam should not oppress women, and are pressing to improve women's rights within the faith.

Since the fall of communism in the late 1980s, life has become harder for many women in Eastern Europe. Some take on hazardous work to support themselves and their families. The woman pictured above is handling coils of asbestos, which is an extremely toxic material.

Perhaps the greatest shift throughout the 20th century was in women's, and men's, expectations. By the end of the century, whether or not they called themselves **feminists**, most women in the West expected equal rights in all areas of life. However, for millions of women around the world, the struggle for equal rights – as well as for basic human needs such as food, shelter, education and healthcare – continues into the 21st century.

Still a long way to go...

An official United Nations report in 1980 stated: 'Although women are fifty per cent of the world adult population, they comprise one third of the official labour force, perform nearly two thirds of all working hours, receive only one tenth of world income, and own less than one per cent of world property.'

Timeline

1902	Women in Australia gain the vote, nine years after women in New Zealand
1900–1914	Suffragists campaign for women's votes in the USA, Britain and around the world
1903	British suffragists form the Women's Social and Political Union to fight for women's votes
1914	Outbreak of World War I
1915	Women's International League for Peace and Freedom formed at peace conference at The Hague
1916	Margaret Sanger opens the first birth-control clinic in the USA
1917	Russian Revolution: women's rights improve in the new Soviet Union
1918	End of World War I.
	British women over the age of 30 gain the vote.
1920	Women in the USA gain the vote.
	Women first allowed to compete in the Olympic Games.
1928	All women gain the vote in Britain at the same age as men (21)
1933	Adolf Hitler's Nazi Party elected to power in Germany, with many women's votes
1939	Outbreak of World War II
1941	Conscription for war work introduced for British women
1945	End of World War II.
	Women in France gain the vote.
1947	India and Pakistan win independence from British rule, with women's support
1948	Universal Declaration of Human Rights adopted by the United Nations
1949	Communist Party takes control of China. Women's rights improve.
	Simone de Beauvoir publishes *The Second Sex* in France.
1955–1967	Women active in the US Civil Rights movement, campaigning for equal rights for people of all races
1960	Sirimavo Bandaranaika of Sri Lanka is the first woman in the world to be elected as prime minister.
	The contraceptive pill becomes available.
1962	Algeria achieves independence from French rule, with women's support
1965	Civil Rights Act ends segregation in the USA
1966	The National Organization for Women formed in the USA.
	The Women's Liberation movement flourishes.
1967	Abortion becomes legal under certain conditions in Britain
1971	Women in Switzerland gain the vote
1972	Equal Rights Amendment adopted by US Congress, although it is never ratified
1973	Roe vs Wade sets US legal precedent allowing abortion in very limited circumstances
1975	United Nations women's conference launches the UN Decade for Women
1979	Convention on Elimination of All Forms of Discrimination Against Women (CEDAW) adopted by the United Nations.
	But some governments, including the USA, refuse to sign up.
	Margaret Thatcher elected Prime Minister in Britain.
1980	Petra Kelly becomes chairperson of the Green Party in Germany, the first woman to head a German political party
1980s	Women campaign against American nuclear weapons stationed in Europe, Australia and North America
1984	Arson and bomb attacks on US abortion clinics rise steeply
1988	Clause 28 introduced in Britain, banning teaching about homosexuality in schools
1989	Fall of communism begins in the Soviet Union and Eastern Europe: life becomes harder for many women
1990	Aung San Suu Kyi elected as leader of Burma, though she is not allowed to govern
1994	Women ordained as Anglican priests in the Church of England
1995	United Nations women's conference in Beijing: Global Platform for Action on women's rights.
1996	The Taliban, Islamic fundamentalists, gradually take control in Afghanistan, undermining women's rights
1997	Labour government elected to power in Britain with 101 women MPs; at 24 per cent, the highest proportion in British history.
	Mary Robinson, former president of Ireland, becomes the UN High Commissioner for Human Rights.
	Madeleine Albright becomes US Secretary of State.
1999	The G8 group of powerful western governments promise to cancel debts totalling $100 billion for some of the world's poorest countries

Further reading

Books: History

Finding Out about Women in Twentieth Century Britain. Sarah Harris, BT Batsford Ltd, 1989

Women's Rights: Changing Attitudes, 1900-2000. Kaye Stearman, Wayland and Amnesty International, 1999

A Century of Women. Sheila Rowbotham, Penguin Books, 1997

Women who Achieved Greatness. Cathie Cush, Raintree Steck–Vaughan, 1995

Women in India and Pakistan, The struggle for independence from British rule. Rozina Visram, Cambridge University Press, 1992

Women's War, the Home Front. Fiona Reynoldson, Wayland 1991

Atlas of the 20th Century. Lisa Miles and Mandy Ross, Usborne Publishing, 1996

Women and Human Rights. K Tomasevski, Zed Books, 1993

The State of Women in the World Atlas. Joni Seager, Penguin Reference, 1997

People's Century volumes 1 and 2. Godfrey Hodgson, BBC Books, 1995/6

100 Greatest Women. Michael Pollard, Dragon's World, 1995

Feminism for Beginners. Susan Watkins, Marisa Rueda and Mata Rodriguez, Icon Books, 1992

Feminism for Teenagers. Sophie Grillet, Piccadilly Press, 1997

Board-game

Who is She? London Union of Youth Clubs, Girl's Fund, 64 Camberwell Rd, London SE5 0EN, UK, 1993

Video

The Moving Pictures Bulletin, issue 24, March 1998 Available from Television Trust for the Environment, TVE Centre, Prince Albert Rd, London NW2 4RZ, UK

Websites

The Women's Library (formerly the Fawcett Library) at London Guildhall University, UK www.lgu.ac.uk/fawcett

The Feminist Library, London, UK www.gn.apc.org/womeninlondon/fl

Jessie Street National Women's Library, Sydney, New South Wales, Australia www.jessiestreetwomenslibrary.com e-mail: jsnwl@cityofsydney.nsw.gov.au

Schlesinger Library, Cambridge, Massachusetts, USA www.radcliffe.edu/schles

Equal Opportunities Commission, Manchester, UK www.eocni.org.uk

Glossary

abortion ending a pregnancy, usually in the first few months

androgynous something that is not defined by its sex; in fashion, clothing that can be worn by both men and women

anorexia a psychological disorder where the person refuses to eat

apartheid the system in South Africa where blacks and other non-whites were kept apart from whites, and deprived of civil rights and basic freedoms such as the right to vote, to travel freely and to choose where to live. The apartheid system was introduced from 1948 and ended in 1994

birth control see contraception

boycott refusing to take part in an action, as a form of protest

civil rights the rights of a citizen to personal freedom, including the right to vote, and sexual and racial equality

Cold War the struggle for global power between the USA and its allies and the Soviet Union and its allies at its height in the 1950s and 60s; it ended in the 1990s

colony an area and its people ruled from another country

communism a political system where the state owns all land and factories, and provides for people's needs

conscription compulsory enrolment for military or other service

contraception, contraceptive birth control, such as a condom or the pill, which allows people to choose whether or when to have children

developing countries countries, mostly in the southern hemisphere, which have not yet developed their full economic or industrial potential, often as a result of slavery, colonialism, debt or corruption

discrimination to treat people differently (usually worse), because of their sex, race or other reason

divorce to end a marriage

domestic service working as a servant in someone else's (usually a wealthy person's) house

domestic violence violence at home, usually, but not always, male violence against a woman

divorce to end a marriage

dowry money or goods paid by the bride's family to the husband's family when a marriage takes place

feminism a movement supporting women's rights and equality. The modern feminist movement began towards the end of the 19th century, alongside the women's suffrage movement. 'Second wave feminism' grew in the 1970s and 80s, following on from the Women's Liberation movement.

fundamentalist abiding by the strict rules and traditions of a particular religion

globalization the flow of goods, services, money, people, images and information across national borders

Great Depression period of world-wide unemployment and poverty after the Wall Street Crash of 1929

house arrest forced against one's will to remain in one place, often the home, which then becomes a prison

human rights the right of every man, woman and child to live free from fear of persecution, discrimination, injustice or violence because of their race, sex, language or religion

independence self-rule for a country, or being able to look after oneself

indigenous people the original inhabitants of a region

infant mortality death of very young children, often caused by hunger or disease

in vitro fertilization a medical process in which an egg is fertilized outside the body and then implanted in the mother's womb

literacy the ability to read and write

malnutrition not having enough of the right kinds of food to stay healthy

midwife healthcare worker, usually a woman, who has medical training to help women give birth safely

migrant someone who travels from one area or country to another

multinational corporation a huge business that is run for profit, and which trades and manufactures in many countries

pension payment made by government or other organization to someone who has retired from work due to age, illness or disability

propaganda publicity that is used to make people believe in something

refugee someone who flees their homeland to escape persecution

revolution a dramatic change; also refers to the overthrow of a ruler or government by a mass action of the people

secular affairs that do not include spiritual or religious matters

segregation separateness or being kept apart

slavery when a person is bought, sold or owned by another person

suffrage the right to vote in elections

suffragette or **suffragist** someone who supports the right to vote. Suffragettes were more extreme in their actions and resorted to acts of violence, like window smashing, to draw attention to their cause. Suffragists were more moderate.

superpower the most powerful states in the world. In most of the post-war era this means the Soviet Union and the United States but now the US is the only superpower.

sweatshops describes poor working conditions where people work in an overcrowded and often unhealthy environment for very low pay

trade union an organization of workers campaigning for better wages and conditions

United Nations (UN) an international organization of governments of independent states. The UN was set up in 1945 after World War II, aiming to promote understanding and peace between nations of the world.

welfare system a system set up by a government to make sure everyone gets education, healthcare, and enough money to live on

West, Western countries political (rather than geographical) name for the rich, industrialized countries of western and northern Europe, North America, Australia and New Zealand

Index